Sharks

Patricia Kendell

RAINTREE
STECK-VAUGHN
PUBLISHERS

A Harcourt Company

Austin   New York
www.raintreesteckvaughn.com

in the wild

**Alligators   Chimpanzees   Dolphins   Elephants
Gorillas   Grizzly Bears   Leopards   Lions
Pandas   Polar Bears   Sharks   Tigers**

Published by Raintree Steck-Vaughn Publishers, an imprint of Steck-Vaughn Company

Library of Congress Cataloging-in-Publication Data is available upon request

ISBN 0-7398-5498-4

Printed in Hong Kong. Bound in the United States.

1 2 3 4 5 6 7 8 9 0 LB 07 06 05 04 03 02

Photograph acknowledgments:
Ardea London Ltd 18 (Don Hadden), 12 & 20 (Ralf Kiefner), 13 & 24 (Ken Lucas), 7 (Pat Morris), 14 (Douglas David Seifert), 29 (Mark Spencer), 3 (third), 6, 16, 23, 25 & 26 (Ron & Valerie Taylor), 19 & 32 (Valerie Taylor); BBC 5 (Michael Pitts), 4 (Bruce Rasner/Rotman); FLPA 1 & 17 (Mammal Fund Earthviews), 8 (D P Wilson); NHPA 3 (fourth) & 21 (Mark Bowler); Oxford Scientific Films 9; Still Pictures 11 (Yves Lefevre), 3 (first & second), 10, 15, 22, 28 (Jeffrey Rotman).

All instructions, information, and advice given in this book are believed to be reliable and accurate. All guidelines and warnings should be read carefully, and the author, packager, editor, and publisher cannot accept responsibility for injuries or damage arising out of failure to comply with the same.

Contents

Where Sharks Live

Sharks live in the seas around the world. Some, like this strange megamouth shark, spend much of their time in the **depths** of the sea.

The basking shark can live in deep water, but comes to shallow water near the coast in summer.

The Shark Family

Sharks belong to the fish family. There are about 400 different types. This whale shark is one of the biggest fish in the sea.

Others, like this dogfish shark, are only
3.3 feet (1 meter) long.

Baby Sharks

Some sharks hatch from eggs laid in egg purses, like these dogfish. Most sharks hatch from eggs inside their mother. Then they are born, like humans.

When they are born, baby sharks look like
miniature adult sharks. Their mother does not
care for them—they must look after themselves.

Finding the Way

Sharks can see, hear, smell, taste, and touch.
This hammerhead shark has a very good view
of the sea all around!

Sharks can easily **detect** movements made in the water, even if the **prey** is a long way off.

On the Move

The great white shark
pushes through the water,
flicking its big forked tail
from side to side.

The leopard shark is very **flexible**.
It can turn around in small places.

Teeth and Food

The sand tiger shark has long curved teeth, which it uses to **snare** fish and **squid**.

The basking shark swims slowly, using its mouth to catch lots of small plants and animals.

Out of Sight

Angel sharks hide in the sand on the seabed,
waiting to snap up a passing fish.

The great white shark's dark back and light underside help to **disguise** it in the water.

Hunter Sharks

Sharks like the great white are powerful hunters.
They can eat a whole seal in one meal.

18

When great whites find a prey, they speed up
and close in.

In for the Kill!

The great white shark's huge jaws open wide,
showing its many saw-like teeth.

This shark is being fed bait, so scientists can see how it eats. As they snap up prey, great whites roll their eyes back into their head to stop them from being scratched.

Shark Attack!

Sharks do sometimes attack and kill people,
but this is very rare.

If great whites do attack, it is usually because they mistake people on surfboards for seals or turtles.

Threats

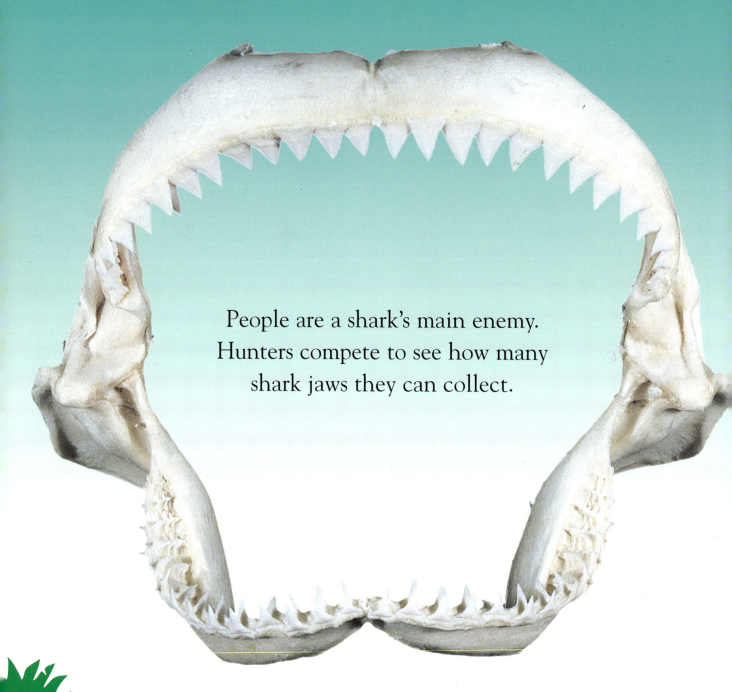

People are a shark's main enemy.
Hunters compete to see how many
shark jaws they can collect.

Sharks are also killed for their meat, fins, skin, and liver oil. Shark teeth are made into jewelry.

Sharks in Danger

Sharks get caught in nets that are set to catch other fish or to protect surfers and swimmers.

All sharks will suffer if the sea is **polluted**,
poisoning the animals that they eat.

Protecting Sharks

Scientists need to find out more about sharks,
so that we will know the best way to protect them.

Countries such as South Africa, the U.S., and Australia have already made laws to stop people from killing sharks like this Caribbean reef shark.

Further Information

ORGANIZATIONS TO CONTACT

National Wildlife Federation
11100 Wildlife Center Drive
Reston, VA 20190-5362
(800) 822-9919
http://www.nwf.org/kids/

World Wildlife Fund
1250 24th Street, N.W.
P.O. Box 7180
Washington, D.C. 20077-7180
http://www.worldwildlife.org/fun/kids.cfm

Discovery KIDS
Discovery Communications
7700 Wisconsin Avenue
Bethesda, MD 20814
(301) 986-0444
kids.discovery.com/KIDS/adv_sharks.html

BOOKS

Bright, Michael. *Sharks*. Chicago, IL: Lorenz Books, 2000.

Harman, Amanda. *Sharks (Endangered! Series)*. Chicago, IL: Benchmark Books, 1997.

Llewellyn, Claire. *My Best Book of Sharks*. Boston, MA: Kingfisher, 1999.

Robinson, Claire. *Sharks (Really Wild Series)*. Westport, CT: Heinemann, 1999.

WEBSITES

Most young children will need adult help when visiting websites. Those listed have child-friendly pages that could be bookmarked.

www.worldwildlife.org/oceans/oceans.cfm
This website includes information about

Glossary

basking sharks.

www.wildlifetrusts.org.uk
Search here for information about basking sharks off the coast of Corrnwall.

www.flmnh.ufl.edu/fish/kids
The site of the Florida Museum of Natural History has information for children about why sharks are in danger, and how to avoid shark attacks.

http://dsc.discovery.com
The video sequence about sharks is worth a look.

www.enchantedlearning.com
This site has lots of information, presented in a child-friendly way, plus activities.

depths – (DEPTHS) the deepest parts of the sea.

detect – (di-TEKT) to find out. A shark has a special sense that helps it to find prey in the sea.

disguise – (diss-GIZE) to use an appearance to hide.

flexible – (FLEK-suh-buhl) able to bend very easily.

miniature – (MIN-ee-uh-chur) looking the same, but much smaller.

polluted – (puh-LOOT-ed) spoiled by harmful chemicals or gases.

prey – (PRAY) an animal hunted by another animal for food.

snare – (SNAIR) to trap.

squid – (SKWID) sea creatures with ten tentacles.

Index